Introduction

As a cake decorator, one of the most exciting the run-up to Christmas is thinking of a new and original cake design for the Christmas tea table. The blend of age-old traditions and modern customs conjures up all sorts of ideas for cake designs, each one with its own special story to tell.

Merry Christmas Cakes is a collection of cake designs that each capture a small part of Christmas, from the traditional to the novelty. As I developed the design for each cake, I tried to make each one as fun and as colourful as possible along the way.

The twelve cakes in this book range from simple designs for the novice sugarcrafter to more adventurous projects for the advanced. Whatever design you choose for your Christmas cake - perhaps the Snowboarding Snowmen out on the slopes, a cute pair of Mistletoe Mice, or a trio of Carol Singers on a cold winter's evening – Merry Christmas Cakes has something to suit any Christmas tea table.

To make your Christmas cake extra special, you can add your own unique, personal touches such as inscribing a name on a sugar gift label, making your own child's favourite toy, or even featuring sugar models of your family members on your cake! Once you've mastered the basics of modelling in sugar, making your Christmas cake should be just as enjoyable as the festivities themselves.

I've really enjoyed putting together the designs for Merry Christmas Cakes - I hope you have as much fun modelling with sugar as I do.

Jan
x

Jan Clement-May

To Mum and Dad for all the years of encouragement.

*A special thank you to Beverley, Jenny, Clare, Sarah and Franco
for giving me the opportunity to fulfil a dream.*

First published in September 2004 by b. Dutton Publishing Limited,
Alfred House, Hones Business Park, Farnham, Surrey, GU9 8BB.

Copyright: Jan Clement-May 2004

ISBN: 0-9532588-9-0

All rights reserved.

Publisher: Beverley Dutton

Editor: Jenny Stewart

Editorial Assistant: Clare Porter

Design: Sarah Richardson

Design Assistant: Francisco Caamano

Photography: Alister Thorpe

Printed in Spain

Contents

Projects

Materials

Virtually all of the materials used to cover and decorate the cakes in this book are edible, with the exception of one or two inedible items such as wires. All of the materials listed below are required for most if not all of the projects and are available from your local sugarcraft shop.

Marzipan

After spreading a thin layer of apricot glaze over your rich fruitcake, it can be covered with marzipan. For the best texture and taste, always use marzipan with a high almond content (at least 23.5%) and a smooth texture. You can make your own marzipan, but I find it quicker and easier to use a ready-to-use paste such as Squires Kitchen Marzipan.

Sugarpaste

I have used ready-made sugarpaste as a cake covering throughout this book. Again, you can make your own sugarpaste, but it is much quicker to use ready-made paste. Always knead the paste before use and keep any paste you have opened but are not using sealed in a plastic food-grade bag to prevent it from drying out. Sugarpaste is available in a range of colours and you can also use paste food colours to colour white sugarpaste as required (see opposite).

SK Mexican Modelling Paste (MMP)

MMP is available in a range of 12 colours which are ready to use. To create further colours, MMP colours can be blended together or paste food colour can be added (as with sugarpaste). MMP is ideal for novelty modelling as it holds its shape well, has a smooth texture and dries soft enough to eat.

White, Flesh, Teddy Bear Brown, Sunshine, Soft Apricot, Poppy, Rose, Pale Mint, Sky Blue, Wisteria, Slate Grey, Cream Celebration (not pictured).

SK Sugar Florist Paste (SFP)

SFP is a stronger paste than sugarpaste or MMP which means it can be rolled out very thinly without tearing. This makes it ideal for making sugar flowers and leaves such as holly.

Edible Food Colours

Food colours are available in paste, dust and liquid form, but I have only used SK Paste and Dust Colours in this book. Paste colours can be added to sugarpaste, Mexican Modelling Paste, Sugar Florist Paste, or any other similar sugar modelling medium. To colour sugarpaste, etc. using paste colour, dip a cocktail stick into the colour, add it to a small amount of the sugarpaste to be coloured and blend thoroughly. Blend this piece into the rest of the sugarpaste to be coloured. Continue to add small amounts of paste colour until the required colour is achieved.

If using SK Dust Colour to add a hint of colour, a sheen or a lustre, use a dry, flat brush to apply the colour to firm (but not dry) paste. Dust colours can also be mixed with cooled, boiled water or clear spirit to create an edible paint.

Other materials used throughout this book include

SK Edible Glue – apply to sugar models with an artist's brush. This is an ideal medium to use as it is entirely edible and dries quickly with a transparent finish.

SK Royal Icing – follow the manufacturer's instructions on the pack to make up the mixture, then use the icing as required, e.g. in a piping bag for inscriptions or apply with a palette knife to create a snowy effect (as in Carol Singers).

Icing sugar – keep an icing sugar shaker to hand as it is used to prevent paste from sticking.

Cooled, boiled water – used as a sticking agent, it is essential that tap water is boiled and allowed to cool before being used on a cake. Clear spirit such as gin, vodka or white rum can also be used for this purpose.

Equipment

Each project comes with a list of specific sugarcraft equipment required to complete the cake. However, there are a number of essential items listed here that it is worth having before you start. You may wish to invest in extra tools and equipment such as cutters and veiners as you go.

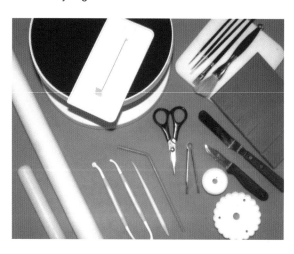

- Cake smoothers
- Kitchen towel
- Modelling tools, including ball tool, bone tool and Dresden tool
- Non-stick (polythene) board
- Non-stick (polythene) rolling pins: large and small
- Paint palette/saucer
- Palette knife
- Pastry brush
- Piping nozzles: various
- Piping bags
- Sharp knife
- Sharp scissors
- SK Brushes: selection for painting, dusting and gluing
- Sugar shaker (for icing sugar)

Modelling Tips

*T*o prevent sugarpaste or MMP from sticking to the board, rolling pin or your hands, use a light dusting of icing sugar.

*W*hen modelling figures or objects from MMP, always allow the paste to firm slightly before assembly. This will ensure that the paste holds its shape. For pieces where the paste has been rolled thinly, such as ribbon loops, a small piece of food-grade foam or kitchen towel can be used to support the paste until dry.

*F*loristry wires are used for items such as the halos for the Carol Singers and Rudolph's antlers in Santa's on his Way! However, you must remember to remove not only the wires, but also the paste in which the wires are inserted (usually the head).

*T*o add extra support to a figure's head, whether it be a person, animal or teddy bear, insert a short length of raw, dried spaghetti into the body and push the head over it. Use a little edible glue to secure the head in place. Remember to remove the spaghetti before the cake is eaten.

*I*f only small items on a cake are made from black paste, such as a teddy's nose, use any leftover pieces of MMP and colour them with SK Jet Black Paste Food Colour.

Alternatively, you can paint the paste colour on using a fine brush.

*I*f you find you do not have the cutters required for a project, you can always make your own templates from a food-grade material such as greaseproof paper.

*T*o save yourself time in the busy run-up to Christmas, make your models in advance and store them in cool, dry conditions until needed.

Basic Techniques

Covering a Cake with Marzipan

1. Spread a thin layer of apricot glaze over the top and sides of the rich fruitcake using a pastry brush.

2. Roll out the marzipan on a non-stick board dusted with icing sugar, then carefully lift the marzipan with the rolling pin and place it over the cake.

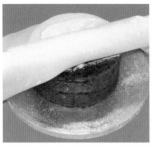

3. Smooth over the surface of the marzipan with your hands and ease it down the sides of the cake.

4. Use a cake smoother to achieve a professional finish and trim away the excess marzipan from the base of the cake using a sharp knife.

5. Place the cake on the required drum. Before covering the cake with sugarpaste, allow the marzipan to firm, preferably overnight.

Covering a Cake and Drum with Sugarpaste (all-in-one)

I have used this method to cover most of the cakes in this book. If you prefer, you can cover the edge of the drum separately to the cake (see opposite).

1. Lightly brush the surface of the marzipanned cake and around the edge of the board with cooled, boiled water (or clear spirit).

2. Roll out a piece of sugarpaste on a non-stick board dusted with icing sugar. The paste must be large enough to cover the cake and drum when rolled out.

3. Carefully lift the paste and position it over the cake and drum.

4. Smooth the paste with your hands, then with a smoother. The paste should come down the sides of the cake and continue onto the board.

5. Use a cake smoother to achieve a professional finish and trim away the excess sugarpaste from around the edge of the board using a sharp knife in a downward motion.

6. Allow the paste to firm, preferably overnight, before adding any decoration.

Covering a Cake Drum

Method 1: To cover a cake drum (as in Pile of Presents, pages 36 to 39), lightly brush the surface of the drum with cooled, boiled water; this will help the paste stick to the drum. Roll out a piece of sugarpaste on a non-stick board dusted with icing sugar, position over the drum, then smooth the surface with a smoother. Cut away the excess paste from around the edge of the board using a sharp knife in a downward motion.

Method 2: To cover the edge of a cake drum after the cake has been positioned, roll out a long strip of sugarpaste and cut a straight edge along one side. Brush the edge of the drum with cooled, boiled water, then position the paste on the drum with the straight edge butting up against the cake. Smooth and trim as usual.

Trimming a Board with Ribbon

1. Cut a piece of 15mm width ribbon a couple of centimetres longer than the circumference of the cake drum.

2. Apply non-toxic glue to the edge of the drum, making sure that the glue does not come into contact with the sugarpaste on the board or cake.

3. Secure the ribbon to the edge of the drum, keeping the join at the back of the cake.

9

Snowboarding Snowmen

Materials

15.5cm and 20.5cm (6" and 8") round fruitcakes

1.5kg (3lb 5oz) SK Marzipan

Sugarpaste: 100g ($3^1/_2$oz) green, 2kg (4lb 6oz) white

Small amount SK Royal Icing

SK Mexican Modelling Paste (MMP): 10g ($^1/_3$oz) each of Poppy, Sky Blue, Slate Grey, Sunshine, Teddy Bear Brown, 200g (7oz) White

SK Food Colour Pen: Blackberry

SK Edible Glue

Raw spaghetti

Equipment

30.5cm (12") round cake drum

1m (40") pale blue ribbon

Bone tool (PME)

Dresden tool (JC)

Piping nozzle: no. 1

Piping bag

Method

Covering the Cakes

1. Stack the smaller cake on top of the larger cake and position off-centre on the cake drum.

2. Cut down the sides of both cakes to make a slope. Use the cut-off pieces to form the peak of the

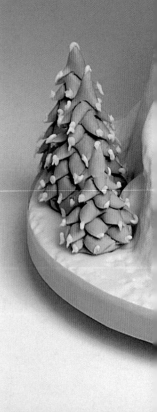

These fun-loving snowmen
are making the most of the
winter weather and have
taken to the slopes on
snowboards!

  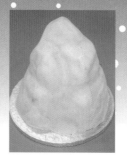 

mountain and other bumps to give an uneven surface. Stick the pieces in place with apricot glaze.

3. Brush the cake surface with apricot glaze and cover with SK Marzipan. Roll two sausages of marzipan and build up the sides of the snow run. Mould the marzipan with your fingers, smoothing it into the marzipan layer beneath. Set aside to dry for 24 hours.

Snow

1. Brush the marzipanned cake and cake drum with clear alcohol or cooled, boiled water. Roll out approximately 1.8kg (4lb) of white sugarpaste and cover the cake and board. Cut away any excess paste and smooth down any joins with your hands. Push the sugarpaste into any crevices – remember that it does not matter how rough the surface is because it is supposed to look like snow! If desired, use the bone tool to make more indentations in the paste.

2. Use the larger end of the bone tool to create long run marks from the top of the mountain, down the side and over the board.

Trees

1. Divide the green sugarpaste into six pieces, varying the sizes to create smaller and larger trees. Mould each piece in your hands to create a cone.

2. Push the thicker end of the Dresden tool up the centre of the cone from the base. Starting at the top of the tree, use a fine pair of scissors to make incisions and lift the paste slightly to form branches.

3. Using SK Edible Glue, attach the trees onto the cake, arranging them as required.

Snowmen

1. Divide the White MMP into four pieces for the snowmen. Divide each of these pieces into different sections: roll a large pear shape piece for the body, a ball for the head and two sausages for arms. Do not stick the pieces together yet. Push a short piece of raw spaghetti into the neck area to support the head.

2. Mix a pinch of Poppy MMP with a tiny piece of Sunshine MMP to make an orange colour. Divide into four and shape into pointed noses. Mark the top with the edge of a knife and attach to the head using SK Edible Glue.

3. Mark the eyes onto each snowman using an SK Blackberry Food Colour Pen.

4. Make a different coloured snowboard for each snowman by simply rolling a sausage of MMP and flattening it with a rolling pin. Glue a snowman body to each snowboard.

Scarves and Hats

1. To make a scarf, roll out a small piece of MMP in the colour of your choice and cut out two strips. (For the paler colours, blend one of the MMP colours with White MMP.) Cut the tassels into one end of each strip using a sharp knife. Flatten a tiny ball of paste between your fingers for the knot and make a small strip to go around the neck.

2. Attach the piece of paste around the neck first, then add the first strip, followed by the flattened ball, and then the second strip.

3. Fix the arms into place with SK Edible Glue, then push the head over the spaghetti stick.

4. To make the bobble hats, roll out a cone of MMP and thin the pointed end slightly. Roll out a thin strip for the brim and mark a ribbed effect with the back of a knife. Attach the cone, then the brim to the snowman's head using SK Edible Glue. Shape it as required, and finally attach a small ball to the end.

5. To make the baseball hats, roll out a round disc shape to fit over the top of the head and attach with SK Edible Glue. For the peak, make a crescent shape and fix to the back or front of the cap.

To Finish

1. Place some SK Royal Icing in a piping bag with a no. 1 piping nozzle. Pipe a little icing onto the end of all the branches of the trees for a completed snow scene.

2. Attach pale blue ribbon to the board with non-toxic stick glue.

Presents Under the Christmas Tree

Materials

15cm (6") square fruitcake

500g (1lb 1oz) SK Marzipan

Sugarpaste: 150g (5oz) green, 600g (1lb 5oz) red

Small amount SK Royal Icing

SK Mexican Modelling Paste (MMP): 50g ($1^3/_4$oz) Flesh, 50g ($1^3/_4$oz) Sky Blue, 50g ($1^3/_4$oz) Sunshine,150g (5oz) Teddy Bear Brown, 50g ($1^3/_4$oz) White

SK Food Colour Pen: Blackberry

SK Paste Food Colours: Blackberry, Rose

SK Edible Glue

Raw spaghetti

Equipment

20.5cm (8") square cake drum

50cm (20") ribbon: green

Star cutter (FMM)

Sugar shaper

Bone tool (PME)

Dresden tool (JC)

Piping nozzle: no. 2

Piping bag

Dowelling rod

Drinking straw

It's Christmas eve and Santa's left the presents under the tree - this novelty design will add a splash of colour to any Christmas tea table.

Method
Covering the Cake

1. Cover the cake with marzipan, then place it towards the back of the cake drum and set aside to dry for 24 hours.

2. Cover the cake and board with red sugarpaste.

Teddy Bear

1. Make a teddy from approximately 50g (1³/₄oz) of Teddy Bear Brown MMP. Start by making the body and insert a short length of raw spaghetti into the neck. Position at the front of the tree and secure in place.

2. Add the arms and legs, marking the paws with the blade of a knife or a Dresden tool.

3. Make the head from a ball of paste, then add a snout and ears. Finally, attach a black nose and mark on the features. Push the head over the spaghetti at the neck and secure with a little SK Edible Glue.

Christmas Tree

1. Insert a plastic dowelling rod into the cake towards the back so that it protrudes from the surface of the cake.

2. Make a large cone from the green sugarpaste. Cut into the paste with sharp scissors, making sure you cut all the way round the cone. Whilst you are cutting, push the rounded end of the Dresden tool underneath the paste for extra support.

3. Brush the dowelling rod with SK Edible Glue, position the Christmas tree over the rod and ease the paste down.

Toy Box

Make a cuboid from 100g (3¹/₂oz) of Teddy Bear Brown MMP for the toy box. Mark the lid with a knife. Secure to the top of the cake beside the tree using SK Edible Glue.

Rag Doll

1. Roll out a long, thin sausage of Flesh MMP for the doll's legs and bend in half. Colour 150g (5oz) of White MMP pink using a little SK Rose Paste Food Colour. Take a tiny piece of pink paste and make the shoes. Secure to the feet with SK Edible Glue. Drape the legs over one corner of the cake.

16

2. Shape approximately 50g (1³/₄oz) of the pink paste into a ball for the torso and position at the top of the legs.

3. Roll out another 50g (1³/₄oz) of pink MMP and, using the riveted end of the Dresden tool, roll over the edges to soften and frill the base of the skirt. Gather the top and pinch to form pleats in the paste. Attach in place over the legs and at the base of the torso using SK Edible Glue.

4. Roll out two long sausages of Flesh MMP for the arms. Slightly flatten at one end for the hands and make a small cut for the thumb. Secure to the body at the shoulders, positioning one arm over the toy box and one across the body.

5. Roll an egg-shaped ball of Flesh MMP for the doll's head. Push the end of a drinking straw into the paste, about two thirds of the way down, to create the mouth. Use the end of a strand of spaghetti to mark the dimples and the eyes. Position the head on top of the torso resting on the toy box and secure with SK Edible Glue.

6. Roll two small balls of Flesh MMP and push the smaller end of the bone tool into each one to make the ears. Secure to the head with SK Edible Glue. Add a small ball of paste for the nose and tiny balls of black coloured MMP in the eyeholes.

7. Soften the Sunshine MMP with a little white vegetable fat. Place the softened paste into a sugar shaper with the multi hole disc and extrude lengths of paste for the hair. Secure each length of hair to the doll's head using the pointed end of the Dresden tool, arranging the hair in all directions. Make a short tuft at the top for the fringe.

17

To Finish

1. Using any remaining MMP, make presents to decorate the cake and board. Make long strips of paste for the ribbons and curl around a tool or the end of a paintbrush.

2. Write 'TOYS' on the lid of the toy box using an SK Blackberry Food Colour Pen.

3. Pipe small dots of royal icing around the sides of the cake and onto the base board.

4. Secure green ribbon around the edge of the cake drum with a non-toxic glue stick.

Tree Decoration

1. Extrude a long piece of Sunshine MMP through the sugar shaper to decorate the tree, attach at the top of the tree and wind around to the bottom. Repeat with softened White MMP. Roll out the remaining Sunshine MMP and cut out a star for the top of the tree. Secure in place with SK Edible Glue.

2. Roll small balls of Sky Blue and Poppy MMP for the baubles and glue in place on the branches.

Candy Canes

Roll out two sausage shapes from Poppy and White MMP, each one approximately 13cm (5") long. Glue the two lengths to each other using SK Edible Glue, then twist together. Neaten off the ends and make a hook shape. Secure in place on the cake with SK Edible Glue.

Ice Castle

Materials

4" (10cm), 6" (15cm) and two 20.5cm (8") round fruitcakes

1.7kg (3lb 12oz) SK Marzipan

2.5kg (5lb 8oz) sugarpaste: white

SK Mexican Modelling Paste (MMP): 500g (1lb 1oz) Sky Blue, 800g (1lb 12oz) White

SK Paste Food Colours: Bluebell, Hyacinth

SK Edible Moon Beams Lustre Dust Colour: Sapphire

SK Edible Glue

Equipment

30.5cm (12") cake drum

10cm and 15cm (4" and 6") round cake boards

1m (40") pale blue ribbon

5 dowelling rods

Method

Covering the Cakes

1. Stack both 20.5cm (8") fruitcakes and cut into the side of both cakes from top to bottom on an angle using a sharp knife. This will form the long path and you can reuse the pieces you have cut away to make a thicker path.

2. Glaze and marzipan the carved cakes and set aside to dry. Glaze and marzipan both the smaller cakes and leave to dry on their respective cake boards for 24 hours.

3. Roll out 1.5kg (3lb 5oz) of white sugarpaste and cover the stacked 20.5cm (8") cakes and drum. Smooth down the paste and cut away any excess from around the board.

4. Cover both the other cakes in the same manner with 500g (1lb 1oz) of white sugarpaste.

5. Push the five dowelling rods into the top of the 20.5cm (8") cakes, spacing them equally. Mark and cut down to size at the surface of the cake.

6. Position the 15cm (6") cake and board on top of the stacked cakes, resting the board on the dowelling rods for support. Place the 10cm (4") cake on top of the 15cm (6") cake.

Castle

1. Mix together 300g (10oz) of White MMP with the same amount of white sugarpaste. Thinly roll out approximately 200g (7oz) of the paste and cut into four equal squares, making sure that the sides are taller than the 10cm (4") cake.

2. Using a sharp knife, make small incisions at the top of

19

each square. Brush the back of each square with SK Edible Glue and secure into position around the 10cm (4") cake, cutting away any overlaps. Dust with SK Sapphire Moon Beams Lustre Dust using a no. 10 SK Brush.

3. To make the turrets, roll out four equal amounts of the same paste, about 50g (1³/₄oz) each, into long sausages. The towers should be thicker than the walls and wider at the base. Dust the turrets with SK Sapphire Moon Beams Lustre Dust and secure in place with SK Edible Glue.

4. For the single turret in the centre, take approximately 50g (1³/₄oz) of the sugarpaste/MMP mixture and roll out another tower as before. Dust with SK Sapphire Moon Beams Lustre Dust and fix it on the top of the castle with SK Edible Glue.

5. Use the remaining 150g (5oz) of the paste for the tops of the turrets. Add a very small amount of SK Bluebell Paste Colour to the paste and knead well. Divide into five equal pieces and shape

each one into a cone. Dust with SK Sapphire Moon Beams Lustre Dust and secure in place with SK Edible Glue.

6. Using the blunt edge of a knife, make little indentations in the walls of the castle to represent windows.

Icicle Walls

1. Mix together the rest of the white sugarpaste and White MMP. Add small amounts of the Sky Blue MMP as you are kneading the paste to create a range of tones for each piece.

2. Starting at the top of the 15cm (6") cake, roll out, cut and dust variegated shapes to resemble shards of ice. Fix into position along the flat base of each shape with SK Edible Glue. Make sure that the tips are crisp and pointed and bend them slightly as you work down the cake to the lower pieces.

3. Continue the same process around the 20.5cm (8") cakes and along the sides of the path.

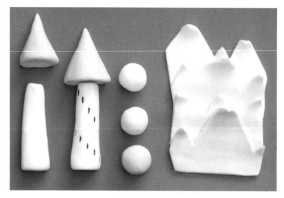

To Finish

1. Using a no. 00 SK Brush, mark the window indents with a little SK Hyacinth Paste Colour mixed with cooled, boiled water. Apply the colour with one brushstroke, being careful not to get colour on the surrounding areas.

2. Fix pale blue ribbon to the cake drum with a non-toxic glue stick.

Crisp, clean ice
shards and a
touch of sparkle
complete this
cool castle – but
it's only cold
outdoors!

Three Tiers for Christmas

Materials

15cm, 20.5cm and 25.5cm (6", 8" and 10") round fruitcakes

1.5kg (3lb 5oz) SK Marzipan

Sugarpaste: 110g (4oz) green, 2kg (4lb 6oz) white

SK Mexican Modelling Paste (MMP): 250g (9oz) Poppy, 100g (3¹/₂oz) Sky Blue, 5g (¹/₅oz) Slate Grey, 100g (3¹/₂oz) Sunshine, 10g (¹/₃oz) Teddy Bear Brown, 60g (2oz) White

SK Sugar Florist Paste (SFP): 150g (5oz) Holly/Ivy, 10g (¹/₃oz) Pale Green, 150g (5oz) White

SK Paste Food Colour: Jet Black

SK Dust Food Colours: Blackberry, Holly/Ivy

SK Bridal Satin Lustre Dust Colour: White Satin

SK Food Colour Pen: Blackberry

SK Edible Glue

SK Confectioners' Glaze

Equipment

20.5cm and 35.5cm (8" and 14") round cake drums

20.5cm (8") round cake board

2m (80") ribbon: white

Large holly cutter (or template) (OP)

SK Great Impressions Medium Holly Veiner

Mistletoe cutter (TT)

Small star cutter

5mm strip cutter (JC)

Ball tool (PME)

Piping nozzle: no. 2

Piping bag

Dowelling rods

CelPad

10cm (4") polystyrene cube

2cm (³/₄") closed curved crimpers (PME)

Method

Covering the Cakes

1. Position the 15cm (6") and 25.5cm (10") cakes onto the 20.5cm (8") and 35.5cm (14") cake drums respectively. Place the 20.5cm (8") cake on the board of the same size.

2. Cover all three cakes with SK Marzipan. Allow to firm for 24 hours.

3. Cover all three cakes with white sugarpaste, also covering the edges of the drums for the small and large cake. Crimp the paste around the edge of both drums.

22

4. Mark the positions for 5 dowelling rods in the largest cake. They should be fairly wide (but not wider than the cake on top) and evenly spaced to support the weight of the upper tiers. Insert the dowels, mark each one 1 or 2mm above the level of the sugarpaste, remove and cut to the required length. Re-insert the dowels into the cake.

5. Carefully place the 25.5cm (8") round cake centrally on top of the large cake, ensuring the dowels take the weight of the cake.

6. Place a no. 2 piping nozzle into a piping bag and fill the bag with royal icing. Pipe a 'snail trail' around the base of each cake and allow to dry.

7. Secure white ribbon around the edges of both cake drums using a non-toxic glue stick, taking care to ensure that the glue does not come into contact with the sugarpaste on the board.

Present Separator

1. Cut another dowelling rod to approximately 17.5cm (7"), i.e. the height of the covered cake plus the height of the polystyrene cube. Push the rod down through the centre of the 25.5cm (8") cake until it reaches the board underneath the cake.

2. Brush SK Edible Glue onto four sides of the polystyrene cube, leaving the top and base. Roll out the Sky Blue MMP, trim to size, i.e. 10cm x 40.5cm (4" x 16"), and cover the sides of the cube. Smooth the join down the side with your fingertip.

3. Take a small amount of Sunshine MMP and roll out into a long strip. Using a 5mm strip cutter, cut out several strips of paste. Using a fine paintbrush, brush SK Edible Glue in diagonal lines on the blue paste, then attach the yellow strips. Trim at the top and base.

4. Mix a little Poppy MMP into 30g (1oz) of White MMP (or use a little SK Poinsettia Paste Food Colour) to create a pale pink colour. Roll out the paste and cut into strips measuring 10cm x 1.3cm (4" x $^1/_2$"). Brush the back of each strip with SK Edible Glue and attach to each side of the present for the ribbon.

5. Push the cube down over the dowelling rod protruding from the middle tier. The rod should come through just above the top of the cube.

Top Tier

1. Roll 110g (4oz) of green sugarpaste into a cone for the Christmas tree, keeping the base flat. Snip into the paste with fine scissors to create branches. Fix the tree into position on the top tier with SK Edible Glue.

2. Roll out a small piece of Sunshine MMP and cut out a small star using a cutter. Fix to the top of the tree with SK Edible Glue.

3. To make the mistletoe for the sides of the cake, mix together 10g ($^1/_3$oz) of Pale Green SFP and 50g (just under 2oz) of White SFP to make a paler green. Roll out the paste thinly and cut out 14 leaves using a mistletoe cutter. Vein each leaf in an SK Great Impressions Medium Holly Veiner, then place each leaf onto a sponge pad and use a ball tool to soften the edges, keeping the tool half on the paste, half on the pad. Pinch the base of each leaf and allow to dry on the CelPad.

4. Roll approximately 18 to 20 balls of White SFP and dust with SK White Satin Lustre Dust. Dust the mistletoe leaves with SK Holly/Ivy Dust Food Colour, then over-dust with the White Satin Lustre Dust. Secure the leaves in pairs around the base of the cake with SK Edible Glue, then add the berries in groups of two or three at the base of the leaves.

Middle Tier

1. To make the candy sticks for the side of the cake, roll out a long sausage of White and Poppy MMP. Twist the two colours together then roll back and forth on a board. Cut into 10cm (4") lengths and hook one end. You will need to make ten candy

25

amount of Teddy Bear Brown MMP. Roll two sticks, making them slightly thicker at one end, and position on the cake near the drum.

Lower Tier

1. To decorate the sides of the lower tier, you will need to make 21 holly leaves. Roll out some Holly/Ivy SFP thinly and cut out leaves using either a cutter or the template provided. Vein each leaf in an SK Great Impressions Medium Holly Veiner and soften the edges in the same way as before using a ball tool. Pinch the base of each leaf and leave on a sponge pad to dry.

2. When dry, colour the holly leaves with SK Holly/Ivy Dust Food Colour, then dust the base of each leaf with SK Blackberry Dust Food Colour. Dip each leaf into SK Confectioners' Glaze and set aside to dry.

3. To make the berries, roll approximately 30-35 balls of Poppy MMP and set aside.

4. Fix each set of three holly leaves to the base of the lower tier with SK Edible Glue, then add four or five berries at the base of the leaves.

Parcels

Using any remaining pieces of MMP, make a number of parcels in different colours and shapes. Make ribbons and bows for each parcel, then secure them to the cake using SK Edible Glue.

sticks altogether. Attach around the side of the middle tier using SK Edible Glue, holding each candy stick in place until it is secure.

2. To make the drum, roll 10g ($^1/_3$oz) of White MMP into a ball. Flatten the ball of paste until it is approximately 2.5cm (1") thick. Colour some Slate Grey MMP black using SK Jet Black Paste Food Colour, roll into a long, thin strip 0.6cm ($^1/_4$") wide and cut in half. Secure a strip around the top and base of the drum. Draw on the strings around the sides of the drum with an SK Blackberry Food Colour Pen. Secure the drum to the cake using SK Edible Glue.

3. Make the drumsticks from a small

26

Santa's on his Way!

Materials

20.5cm (8") square fruitcake

800g (1lb 12oz) SK Marzipan

Sugarpaste: 10g ($^1/_3$oz) chocolate, 160g (5$^1/_2$oz) green, 500g (1lb 1oz) red, 350g (12$^1/_2$oz) white

Small amount SK Royal Icing

SK Mexican Modelling Paste (MMP): 10g ($^1/_3$oz) Rose, 20g ($^3/_4$oz) Slate Grey, 10g ($^1/_3$oz) Sky Blue, 10g ($^1/_3$oz) Sunshine, 300g (10$^1/_2$oz) Teddy Bear Brown

SK Paste Food Colour: Jet Black

SK Metallic Lustre Dust Colour: Antique Gold

SK Food Colour Pen: Blackberry

SK Edible Glue

Raw spaghetti

Equipment

25.5cm (10") round cake drum

1m (40") ribbon: red

Bone tool (PME)

Dresden tool (JC)

Piping nozzle: no. 1

Piping bag

Two 28-gauge floristry wires

Wire cutters

Light brown floristry tape

Method

Covering the Cake Drum

1. Cover the cake drum with 200g (7oz) of the white sugarpaste. Texture the paste using a bone tool to create an uneven, snowy surface.

2. Fix the ribbon to the side of the cake drum with non-toxic glue and set aside to dry.

Carving the Cake

1. Cut the 20.5cm (8") square fruitcake in half to make two oblongs. Cut a section away from one half, approximately 6.5cm (2$^1/_2$") wide (this will form Rudolph's body later).

27

A = Piece for sleigh

B = Piece for sack

C = Piece for Rudolph's body

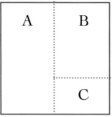

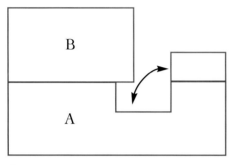

2. Using the diagram as a guide, cut out a piece for the footplate and place this on top of the cake at the front end of the sleigh. Using a sharp knife, carve the cake to shape the front and back of the sleigh.

3. Use the last piece of cake (from the other half) to make the sack. Carve the top and sides of the cake with a sharp knife to create a more rounded shape and make small indentations in the top for the presents. Place this on the back of the sleigh.

4. Shape the small piece of cake that is left into a rounded body for Rudolph, making it slightly bigger at the back.

5. Cover the sleigh, sack and Rudolph's body with marzipan and allow to dry overnight.

6. Position the marzipan-covered sleigh at the back of the board, leaving enough room at the front for Rudolph.

Sack

1. Add some SK Jet Black Paste Colour to the SK Slate Grey MMP to make black. Divide this paste in half and use one piece to cover the top of the sack, smoothing down the edges with your fingers.

2. Roll out 150g (5oz) of Teddy Bear Brown MMP into a long rectangular shape. Wrap the paste around the marzipan, securing at the back with a little SK Edible Glue. Smooth down the edges with your fingers. Cut away any excess paste around the base.

3. Mark the sack with a Dresden tool; this will make it look as though it is full of presents. Slightly roll over the top of the sack.

Sleigh

1. To make the footplate, roll out the remaining black MMP, cut to size and secure in place with SK Edible Glue.

2. Roll out about 50g (1³/₄oz) of red sugarpaste, big enough to cover the back of the sleigh. Cut a rectangular shape and fix into position around the edges with SK Edible Glue.

3. For the front end, roll out about 100g (3¹/₂oz) of red sugarpaste and cut out a longer rectangle to fit from the base of the board to the footplate. Secure with a little SK Edible Glue at the edges. Use a Dresden tool to mark both the front and back pieces with a scroll pattern.

4. Roll out another 150g (5oz) of red sugarpaste and cut a piece to fit the side of the sleigh (see template). Make sure

Children will love this cake – for an extra special touch, you could even add personalised labels on the presents in Santa's sack.

that it matches the front but make an overhang on the back part so that it goes around the back of the sack. Secure in place using SK Edible Glue. Repeat the process for the other side but in a mirror image of the first side.

5. Dust the sleigh with SK Antique Gold Metallic Lustre Dust Colour.

6. Add the snow on and around the sleigh by rolling long pieces of white sugarpaste. Brush SK Edible Glue along the base of the sleigh and fix the snow in place. Push a bone tool down into the MMP, making the same patterns as for the snow on the board. For the snow on the sleigh, mark the paste with a Dresden tool before securing into position over the arches, back and front.

7. Roll out a small piece of white sugarpaste and cut out a rectangle for Santa's plate at the front. Secure in place with SK Edible Glue. Write 'Santa 1' on the panel with an SK Blackberry Food Colour Pen. Using the same pen, draw footprints in the snow.

Trees

Make four trees from 150g (5oz) of green sugarpaste (as described on page 12). Position one on the board at the front and three behind the sleigh, securing into position with SK Edible Glue. Add a little snow on the branches using SK Royal Icing.

Parcels and Presents

Use any left over pieces of MMP and sugarpaste to make a selection of parcels, a ball and some candy sticks (described on page 25). Make a train from Sky Blue MMP, fixing the pieces together with SK Edible Glue. Remember to keep back a small pinch of white, pink and red paste for Rudolph.

Rudolph

1. Cover the body with Teddy Bear Brown MMP. Use a Dresden tool to mark where his hind leg will be.

2. Roll out three small sausages for legs (don't worry; he hasn't lost a leg he's just laying on it!) and secure into position with SK Edible Glue. Smooth the paste into the body to hide the joins. Mark the joints with a Dresden tool.

3. Using chocolate sugarpaste, shape three hooves and press the bone tool on the underneath of each. Affix to the end of each leg.

4. Make the tail from Teddy Bear Brown MMP, secure in place with SK Edible Glue and smooth the join. Mark with a Dresden tool.

5. Shape a small piece of paste for the ruff and neck, attach in place and mark the ruff with a Dresden tool. Push a piece of raw spaghetti into the neck to support the head when it is in place.

6. Reserve a small amount of Teddy Bear Brown MMP for the ears and tuft of hair. Roll the rest into a pear shape for the head and run the blunt side of a knife around the smaller end to mark the mouth. Brush a little SK Edible Glue around the top of the neck and position Rudolph's head in place.

7. Make the reins and noseband from red

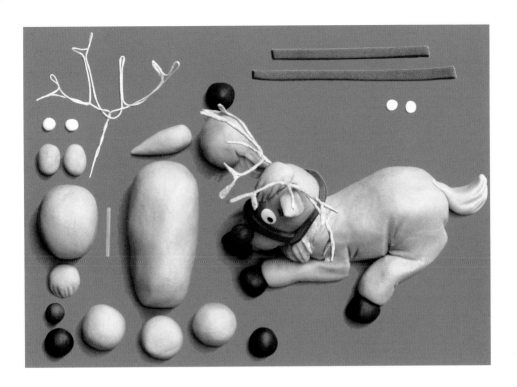

sugarpaste. Secure into place with SK Edible Glue and push a Dresden tool into the joins for a neat finish.

8. Roll a small ball of red sugarpaste for Rudolph's famous nose and secure into place with SK Edible Glue.

9. Roll out two balls of both Teddy Bear Brown and Rose MMP, place on top of each other and pinch between your fingers. Shape into pointed ears and position on either side of Rudolph's head using the larger end of a bone tool.

10. Shape the last piece of Teddy Bear Brown MMP into a tuft of hair and place on Rudolph's head between his ears. Mark with a Dresden tool in the same way as for the tail.

11. Roll out two small balls of white sugarpaste for the eyes and flatten between your fingers. Secure above the noseband and mark the eyeballs and eyebrows with an SK Blackberry Food Colour Pen.

12. Gently place Rudolph at the front of the sleigh and secure to the board with SK Edible Glue. To make the antlers, bend 28-gauge floristry wires into shape and wrap light brown floristry tape around the wires to cover them completely. Push the ends into the head, either side of the hair tuft. As the antlers are made from wire and have been pushed into the head, remember to remove the head and antlers completely before eating the cake.

Mistletoe and Mice

Materials

15.5cm (6") square fruitcake

500g (1lb 1oz) SK Marzipan

Sugarpaste: 500g (1lb 1oz) pale blue

SK Mexican Modelling Paste (MMP): 15g ($\frac{1}{2}$oz) Slate Grey, 100g ($3\frac{1}{2}$oz) White

SK Sugar Florist Paste (SFP): 60g (2oz) each of Pale Green, White

SK Paste Food Colour: Rose

SK Dust Food Colour: Holly/Ivy

SK Bridal Satin Lustre Dust Colours: Chiffon Pink, White Satin

SK Food Colour Pen: Blackberry

SK Edible Glue

Raw spaghetti

Equipment

20.5cm (8") square cake drum

50cm (20") pale blue ribbon

Mistletoe cutter (TT)

Bone tool (PME)

Dresden tool (JC)

CelBoard (CC)

CelPad (CC)

Small CelPic (CC)

26 gauge wires: white

Wire cutters

Floristry tape: pale green

This romantic pair of mice sitting under the mistletoe will have you smiling at Christmas time!

Method
Covering the Cake

1. Place the cake centrally on the cake drum. Brush the cake with apricot glaze and cover with SK Marzipan. Set aside to dry for 24 hours.

2. Cover the cake and drum in pale blue sugarpaste and cut away any excess paste from the board.

3. Secure pale blue ribbon around the drum using a non-toxic glue stick.

Mistletoe

1. Cut 5cm (2") lengths of white wire for the berries and make a hook at one end.

2. Roll some White SFP into small balls for berries. Dip the hooked end of each piece of wire into SK Edible Glue and then push into a ball of paste, securing the wire by gently pinching the SFP around the base. Complete all the wired berries in the same way and set aside to dry on a CelPad.

3. Roll out some Pale Green SFP on a CelBoard until the paste is quite thin. Dip a 12.5cm (5") length of white wire into SK Edible Glue and insert at the thicker end of the sugarpaste. Be careful not to push the wire too far otherwise it may come through the SFP.

4. Place the mistletoe cutter centrally over the wire and cut out a mistletoe leaf. Pull away the excess paste from around the cutter and lift the leaf onto the CelPad.

5. Run the pointed end of the Dresden tool from the top of the leaf to the bottom

to mark the central vein. Run a bone tool around the edge of the leaf to soften the edges. Set aside on the CelPad to dry.

6. Repeat steps 3 to 5 for the other leaves, making as many as required. I have used 11 altogether, but more leaves may be needed if your cake is bigger to keep the mistletoe in proportion.

7. Dust the mistletoe berries with SK White Satin Lustre Dust and tape into small bunches of threes or fours using pale green floristry tape.

8. Dust the base of each leaf with a little SK Holly/Ivy Dust Food Colour to give them some definition and then dust with SK White Satin Lustre Dust.

9. Start taping the end of a white wire with pale green floristry tape and then tape in the leaves. Tape down to form a stem and bring in a bunch of mistletoe berries. To make the mistletoe more authentic, make two or three and maybe even four branches. Tape them in the same manner as the first, joining them at different levels. Finally, tape all the wires together, forming the stem.

Mice

1. Mix together 90g (3oz) of White MMP with 10g ($^{1}/_{3}$oz) of Slate Grey MMP to make a pale grey colour. Divide the paste in half for the two mice.

2. Divide both pieces of paste roughly in half, using one half for each body and the other half for the head, ears, arms, feet and tail. Roll two slightly lengthened

than the grey ones and attach the pink circles to the grey with SK Edible Glue. Pinch the paste between your fingers and secure in place with SK Edible Glue.

7. Bend and shape the mistletoe as desired. Fill a small CelPic with sugarpaste or MMP and insert into the back half of the cake. Push the end of the mistletoe stem into the CelPic and position the mistletoe, bending it over slightly.

pear shapes between your palms for the bodies. Secure them to the cake with SK Edible Glue. Push a small piece of raw spaghetti into the top of each body at the neck to support the head.

3. Roll out four smaller pieces of paste for the back feet, and then indent their toes with the Dresden tool. Secure into position at the bases of both bodies.

4. Roll out four slightly thinner lengths for their arms, marking their fingers with the Dresden tool. Position just below their necks, wrapping their arms around each other.

5. Roll out two balls for their heads and then pull out the paste at one end to form the snout. Roll two tiny balls of pale grey MMP, brush with SK Edible Glue and attach at the pointed end of each head to make two noses. Push each head onto the spaghetti, making sure that the mice are cheek to cheek.

6. Make four circles of the grey paste for the ears. Colour a tiny piece of White MMP pink using a hint of SK Rose Paste Food Colour. Divide the pink paste into four, make four circles slightly smaller

8. Divide the remaining grey sugarpaste in half and roll each piece out to form two tails. Secure at base of the mice, one curling round and the other attached to the mistletoe.

9. Draw both sets of eyes and whiskers onto the mice with the SK Blackberry Food Colour Pen and colour in the noses. Dust the cheeks of one mouse with SK Chiffon Pink Lustre Dust.

To Finish

1. Roll the remaining baby blue sugarpaste into different sized balls and attach around base of cake and on the board. Scatter balls in groups around the top and the base of the mistletoe to hide the CelPic.

2. Dust all the balls with a little SK White Satin Lustre Dust to give a slight sheen.

Pile of Presents

Materials

10cm (4") round fruitcake

15cm and 20.5cm (6" and 8") square fruitcakes

1kg (2lb 3oz) SK Marzipan

Sugarpaste: 250g (9oz) blue, 400g (14oz) cream, 350g (12oz) pale blue, 200g (7oz) pink, 250g (9oz) red, 200g (7oz) yellow

SK Mexican Modelling Paste (MMP): 100g (3^1/$_2$oz) Cream Celebration, 50g (1^3/$_4$oz) Pale Mint, 100g (3^1/$_2$oz) Poppy, 100g (3^1/$_2$oz) Sky Blue, 100g (3^1/$_2$oz) Teddy Bear Brown, 50g (1^3/$_4$oz) White

10g (1/3oz) SK Sugar Florist Paste (SFP): White

SK Paste Food Colour: Jet Black

SK Dust Food Colours: Blackberry, Holly/Ivy

SK Metallic Lustre Dust Colour: Antique Gold

SK Food Colour Pens: Holly/Ivy, Poinsettia

SK Edible Glue

SK Confectioners' Glaze

Equipment

30.5cm (12") square cake drum

1.5m (60") ribbon: blue

7mm strip cutter (JC)

Multi-ribbon cutter (FMM)

Star calyx cutter (TT)

Drinking straw

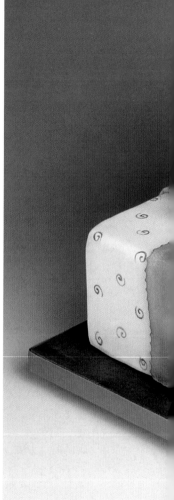

Method
Covering the Cakes

1. Cover the cake drum with blue sugarpaste. Cut away any excess paste around the board edge and set aside to dry.

2. Cut the 20.5cm (8") square cake into three pieces: one 7.5cm (3") cube, one 7.5cm x 12.5cm x 7.5cm (3" x 5" x

This simple design can be personalised so there is a present for every member of the family in their favourite colours.

MERRY CHRISTMAS TO ALL...

3") and one 12.5cm x 20.5cm x 7.5cm (5"x 8" x 3") cuboid.

3. Glaze and marzipan all five cakes and set aside to dry for 24 hours.

Gold Parcel

1. Cover the 15cm (6") square cake with cream sugarpaste.

2. Using the multi-ribbon cutter, take the 4cm (1$^1/_2$") spacers and wavy edge cutter. Roll out the remaining cream sugarpaste and cut two long strips. Cut two smaller strips for the tails of the bow and make an inverted 'V' at one end of each strip. Cut two slightly shorter strips for each loop of the bow and a small, flattened disc for the knot.

3. Brush one side of all the strips with SK Antique Gold Lustre Dust and fix each one in place on the parcel with SK Edible Glue.

4. Mix a small amount of cooled, boiled water or clear alcohol with SK Antique Gold Lustre Dust. Using a no. 0 SK Brush, paint a pattern onto the parcel to represent wrapping paper.

Pink Present

1. Cover the 10cm (4") round cake with pink sugarpaste. Position on the cake board next to the gold parcel.

2. Using an SK Poinsettia Food Colour Pen, draw a simplified blossom pattern onto the sugarpaste.

3. Roll out the White MMP and cut out lengths of ribbons using a 7mm (no. 3) strip cutter. Secure long pieces to the centre of the parcel and twist down the sides and onto the board, fixing in place as you go with SK Edible Glue.

4. Cut the remaining ribbon strips into 5cm (2") pieces and attach the ends together with SK Edible Glue to form loops. Repeat this to make about sixteen loops in total. Allow to firm slightly so that the paste holds its shape.

5. Brush some SK Edible Glue in the centre of the present and attach each loop in turn to form a bow, making sure that one is pushed into the top to hide all the ends.

Blue Parcel

1. Cover the 12.5cm x 20.5cm x 7.5cm (5" x 8" x 3") cake with pale blue sugarpaste, taking care to smooth down the joined areas.

2. Roll out the Sky Blue MMP and cut long strips using a 7mm strip cutter. Position the blue strips diagonally on the parcel and secure with SK Edible Glue. Cut away any excess at the base. Secure the cake to the board with SK Edible Glue.

3. Roll out 50g (1$^3/_4$oz) of Poppy MMP and

cut a long strip using 4cm (1½")
spacers on the ribbon cutter and
straight edge wheels. Fix the strip off-
centre on the parcel, bringing it up and
over the back. Trim away any excess
from the base.

4. For the label, roll out some White SFP
thinly and cut to the shape of a label.
Use the drinking straw to make a hole
for the loop to go through.

5. Roll out a long, thin string of White MMP
and secure it to the top of the parcel
and through the label hole, securing the
label at the same time. Make sure
everything is firmly attached with SK
Edible Glue.

6. Write your chosen inscription on the
label with an SK Poinsettia Food Colour
Pen.

Yellow Box

1. Cover the
7.5cm (3") cube
cake with
yellow
sugarpaste.
Secure to the
top of the gold parcel with SK Edible
Glue.

2. Using SK Holly/Ivy and Poinsettia Food
Colour Pens, mark a holly design on the
sugarpaste.

3. Make a teddy from Teddy Bear Brown
MMP (see 'Presents Under the
Christmas Tree', page 16 for full
instructions). Arrange the limbs so that
the bear is lying on his side and attach
to the top of the present.

Red Present

1. Cover the
final cake
with the red
sugarpaste.

2. Roll out the
Pale Mint MMP and cut approximately
50 stars using a small star calyx cutter.
Stick the stars all over the parcel with
SK Edible Glue.

3. Roll out the remaining Poppy MMP and
once again use the ribbon cutter,
straight edge wheel and spacer to cut a
long strip. Cut two pieces approximately
5cm (2") long and cut a 'V' in the end of
both. Pinch the tops of the strips
together and secure into position with
SK Edible Glue.

4. Cut approximately nine more pieces
from the Poppy MMP, each measuring
4cm (1½") long. Join the ends together
to form loops and position them over
the other two strips in a circular pattern,
finishing with one loop in the centre.
Secure all the loops with SK Edible
Glue.

5. Secure the parcel to the cake drum
behind the yellow box.

To Finish

1. Fix the ribbon to the cake drum using
the non-toxic glue stick.

2. To add a festive touch,
make a sprig of holly (see
instructions on page 26)
and place in one corner
of the board.

39

And a Partridge in a Pear Tree

Materials

10cm, 15cm and 20.5cm (4", 6" and 8") round fruitcakes

1kg (2lb 3oz) SK Marzipan

Sugarpaste: 100g ($3^1/_2$oz) chocolate, 1.5kg (3lb 4oz) cream, 250g ($8^3/_4$oz) green

SK Mexican Modelling Paste (MMP): 75g ($2^3/_4$oz) Flesh, 25g (1oz) Poppy, 25g (1oz) Rose, 20g ($^3/_4$oz) Sky Blue, 25g (1oz) Slate Grey, small amount Soft Apricot, 10g ($^1/_3$oz) Sunshine, 25g (1oz) Teddy Bear Brown, 100g ($3^1/_2$oz) White

SK Paste Food Colours: Edelweiss, Jet Black

SK Edible Metallic Lustre Dust Colour: Antique Gold

SK Food Colour Pen: Blackberry

SK Edible Paint: Gold, Silver

SK Edible Glue

SK Glaze Cleaner (IPA)

Raw spaghetti

Equipment

30.5cm (12") round cake drum

10cm and 15cm (4" and 6") round cake boards

1m (40") gold ribbon

Six-petal daisy cutter (JC)

Alphabet cutter set (JC)

Numeral cutters (JC)

Ball/bone tool (PME)

Dresden tool (JC)

Dowelling rods

8cm (3") wide egg-shaped polystyrene ball

2cm ($^3/_4$") closed curved crimpers (PME)

Floristry tape: brown

Drinking straw

This cake celebrates one of the most loved carols sung at Christmas time, the Twelve Days of Christmas.

Method

Covering the Cakes

1. Position the largest cake centrally on the cake drum and the other two cakes on the respective cake boards. Glaze and marzipan all the cakes and set aside to dry for 24 hours.

2. Roll out 800g (1lb 12oz) of cream sugarpaste and cover the large cake and drum. Crimp the paste around the edge of the drum. Cover the two smaller cakes with cream sugarpaste.

3. Insert four dowelling rods into the largest cake, ensuring they are evenly spaced. Mark each one just above the level of the sugarpaste, remove, cut down to size and re-insert. Gently place the middle cake and board on top of the base cake, making sure the dowelling rods give good support and are covered by the cake. Dowel the middle cake in the same way and place the smallest cake on top.

Letters and Numbers

Roll out the remaining cream sugarpaste and cut out the numbers from 1 to 12 and the letters for the inscription, 'On the twelfth day of Christmas my true love gave to me'. Allow to dry, and then brush the letters and numbers with SK Antique Gold Metallic Lustre Dust Colour. Be careful not to break the pieces as you do this. Position each letter onto the cake sides and attach with SK Edible Glue. Do not attach the numbers at this stage.

Pear Tree

1. Wrap brown floristry tape around a dowelling rod from top to bottom. Push the dowelling rod into the centre of the smallest cake and push the polystyrene ball over the dowelling rod by about 7.5cm (3").

2. Roll out 100g ($3\frac{1}{2}$oz) of green sugarpaste, brush the polystyrene ball with SK Edible Glue and cover the ball with the sugarpaste. Smooth the sugarpaste down with your hands and remove any excess paste from underneath.

3. Reserve about 20g ($\frac{3}{4}$oz) of green sugarpaste for the pears and 10g ($\frac{1}{3}$oz) for the milkmaid's top and roll out the remainder. Make leaves from the sugarpaste with the daisy cutter and, working from the base to the top, use SK Edible Glue and the larger end of the ball tool to secure the leaves to the ball. Make sure you leave enough room for the partridge to go on the top of the tree.

4. Make a tiny bow from Poppy MMP and attach to the tree trunk with SK Edible Glue.

5. Mix a pinch of Slate Grey MMP with some of the reserved green sugarpaste for the pears. Make approximately 11 pears and push the rounded end of a Dresden tool into the base. Dust with SK Antique Gold Metallic Lustre Dust Colour.

6. Position the pears around the tree and one at the bottom of the tree and secure with SK Edible Glue, holding them in place as the glue dries.

7. Make the partridge following the stage photograph and secure on top of the tree.

2 Turtle Doves

Model a turtle dove from MMP following the stage photograph and secure to the top of the middle tier with SK Edible Glue.

3 French Hens

Model a hen from MMP following the stage photograph and secure to the top of the middle tier near the dove.

4 Calling Birds

Model a black bird from MMP following the stage photograph and secure to the top of the middle tier near the hen.

5 Gold Rings

Divide 10g ($^{1}/_{3}$oz) of cream sugarpaste into five balls, push a hole through the middle and flatten down the sides to make a ring. Allow to firm, then paint with SK Edible Gold Paint and clean the brush with the SK Glaze Cleaner straight away. Secure all five rings around the number 5 with SK Edible Glue.

6 Geese a Laying

1. Make a nest for the goose using a mix of SK Teddy Bear Brown MMP and a pinch of Sunshine MMP. Mark the nest with a Dresden tool and fix it to the cake with SK Edible Glue.

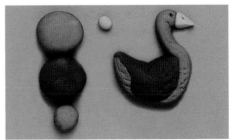

43

2. Make a goose following the stage photograph, and then secure the goose to the nest using SK Edible Glue.

7 Swans a Swimming

1. Using 5g ($^1/_5$oz) of SK Sky Blue MMP mixed with SK Edelweiss Colour Paste to make it lighter, mark the MMP with the Dresden tool to make it look like water. Secure it to the base cake with SK Edible Glue.

2. Make the swan following the stage photograph, then attach the swan to the water using SK Edible Glue.

44

8 Maids a Milking

1. Make two buckets from White MMP. Paint each bucket with SK Edible Silver Paint, leaving the tops white. Attach a bucket to the cake using SK Edible Glue.

2. Make the yoke from chocolate sugarpaste and position on the side of the cake at an angle. Attach the other bucket to the cake with SK Edible Glue with its handle over the hooked end of the yoke.

3. To make the skirt, cut out a triangle shape from Teddy Bear Brown MMP, push your fingers into the bottom of the triangle and pinch the sides. Mark from the top end of the skirt with a Dresden tool. Secure to the cake directly under the yoke.

4. For the shoes, make two triangles from chocolate sugarpaste and fix to the underneath of the skirt with SK Edible Glue.

5. For the pinafore, cut out a triangle from White MMP, cut off the top and score down from top to bottom with a Dresden tool. Fix to the front of the skirt with SK Edible Glue.

6. For the bodice, roll a pear shape from green sugarpaste, cut off at the waistline and secure to the skirt top and the side of the cake with SK Edible Glue. Pinch out slightly between your finger and thumb for the bust.

7. Make the arms from White MMP, mark the elbows with a Dresden tool and bend. Stick into position either side of the bodice with SK Edible Glue. Push the rounded end of the Dresden tool into the ends of the arms to make indents for the hands to go into. Use the other end of the Dresden tool to mark the shoulders.

8. Make the collar and hands and secure in place. Secure one hand over and behind the top of the yoke. Mark up the bodice with a crisscross pattern using an SK Blackberry Food Colour Pen.

9. To make the head, roll approximately 5g ($^1/_5$oz) of Flesh MMP into an egg shape. Push a piece of raw spaghetti into the bodice at the neck and position the head on top, pushing down gently and securing with SK Edible Glue. Use the end of a drinking straw to mark the mouth and mark the dimples and eyes with a piece of raw spaghetti. Add a nose and ears.

10. Make the plaits and fringe from a small amount of Sunshine MMP and mark 'V' shapes down the plaits with the Dresden tool. Fix the plaits and fringe in place using SK Edible Glue.

11. Make the hat from White MMP, making sure that it will fit over her head. Pull each side out slightly and flick up at the ends. Secure into position with SK Edible Glue.

12. Finally, mark the eyes with SK Jet Black Paste Food Colour using a fine brush or an SK Blackberry Food Colour Pen.

45

9 Ladies Dancing

1. Take the Rose MMP and remove enough for the sleeves. Roll the rest on the board with your palms until you have a cone shape. Push down the top so that it is rounded and bend it over slightly. Mark the dress with the Dresden tool, pulling the tool in a curving motion to give the dress movement and lifting the hemline in places. Secure to the base board with SK Edible Glue.

2. Divide the reserved Rose MMP in half for the sleeves, mark them with a Dresden tool and secure into position with SK Edible Glue.

3. Roll a small amount of Flesh MMP around a stick of spaghetti for each arm, leaving a short length protruding at one end. Push this end into the sleeve, then flatten and round the ends for hands.

4. Make the head as before, then make the hair from Sunshine MMP and mould it to the back of her head. Draw the hair down to her neck and around her ears and forehead with a Dresden tool.

Attach a small bun to the back of her head and mark in the same way. For the front curls, roll tiny pieces of SK Sunshine MMP into thin strips, cut to the required length and secure each one to the hair line using SK Edible Glue. Gently curl in different directions using the pointed end of the Dresden tool.

10 Lords a Leaping

1. Push a raw spaghetti stick into the side of the base cake, leaving enough protruding to give support to the lord's body. Make the trousers from cream sugarpaste, mark them with a Dresden tool and push them onto the spaghetti stick at the side of the cake. Fix with SK Edible Glue.

2. For his stockings, roll two sausages of Sky Blue MMP, flatten at one end and fix them to each trouser leg with SK Edible Glue. Make two slightly pointed shoes from Sky Blue MMP and secure to the stockings.

3. Make the waistcoat from Sky Blue MMP, and then add the arms. Add a ruffle to

each sleeve and at the neck, marking with a Dresden tool.

4. Make the head as for the other figures and add white hair. Add curls on the top and sides of his head, then add a ponytail with a bow made from Sky Blue MMP.

11 Pipers Piping

1. Make the piper's legs from approximately 15g ($^1/_2$oz) of chocolate sugarpaste, bend one leg and secure to the board with SK Edible Glue. Make the body and arms in the same way as for the milkmaid using brown paste.

2. Before the arms are fixed in place, make the shoes, belt and shoulder pads from Slate Grey MMP mixed with SK Jet Black Paste Food Colour. Make two oval shapes for shoes, then roll out the rest of the MMP mix and cut into two strips, one for the belt and the other for the band from his shoulder to his waist. Attach with SK Edible Glue. Flatten two small balls of paste for his shoulder pads and attach with SK Edible Glue.

3. Make the piper's head in the same way as before and secure to the body.

4. Make the bagpipes from Poppy MMP and mark the pattern with the Dresden tool. Push three pieces of raw spaghetti into the top of the bagpipes and one underneath. His hands should be fixed to the pipes as if he is playing them. Push a spaghetti stick into his mouth and the other end into the bagpipes.

5. Make the sporran, hair and feather from Teddy Bear Brown MMP, then make the hat and sporran detail from chocolate sugarpaste. Secure all the pieces in place with SK Edible Glue.

12 Drummers Drumming

1. For the drum, roll approximately 10g ($^1/_3$oz) of White MMP into a ball and flatten. Colour some Slate Grey MMP black and make two strips to fit around the top and bottom of the drum. Secure into place with SK Edible Glue and cut off any excess. Secure the drum to the cake board with SK Edible Glue. Roll out two pieces of chocolate sugarpaste

for the drumsticks and fix to the top of the drum with SK Edible Glue.

2. Colour some Slate Grey MMP with SK Jet Black Paste Food Colour for the drummer's legs, shoes and hat. For the legs, roll out a long sausage that gets thinner at each end. Pull each end round to meet and stick the sides together with SK Edible Glue. Cut off the ends to give a straight edge. Use the cut off pieces to make a pair of shoes, then fix these to the legs with SK Edible Glue. Secure the legs and shoes to the lower tier.

3. Make the body and arms from Poppy MMP in the same way as for the milkmaid, omitting the bust!

4. Make the buttons and shoulder pads from White MMP and fix them to the tunic with SK Edible Glue. Mark on the detail with the SK Blackberry Food Colour Pen.

5. Make his head in the same way as the milkmaid, fixing it to a raw spaghetti stick pushed into the top of his body. Draw a strap under his chin with the SK Blackberry Food Colour Pen.

6. Make an oval shape for the hat from the black paste and use your finger and thumb to pull out the edge so the hat fits over the top of his head. Secure with SK Edible Glue.

7. Make the feather from a small oval of White MMP with a ball of Poppy MMP at the base.

To Finish

Attach the numbers to the cake with SK Edible Glue. Finally, secure gold ribbon around the edge of the cake drum.

Say a Little Prayer for Me!

Materials

10cm (4") and two 15.5cm (6") round fruitcakes

400g (14oz) SK Marzipan

Sugarpaste: 500g (1lb 1oz) white

SK Mexican Modelling Paste (MMP): 100g (3$^1/_2$oz) Flesh, 200g (7oz) White

SK Sugar Florist Paste (SFP): 10g ($^1/_3$oz) White

SK Paste Food Colours: Daffodil, Jet Black

SK Metallic Lustre Dust Colour: Antique Gold

SK Mini Silver Balls

SK Edible Glue

Equipment

10" (25.5cm) round cake drum

1m (40") gold ribbon

Garrett frill cutter (OP)

Ball tool (PME)

Dresden tool (JC)

Piping nozzle

Dowelling rod

4cm (1$^1/_2$") polystyrene ball

2cm ($^3/_4$") closed curved crimpers (PME)

24 gauge floristry wire: white

Wire cutters

Tweezers

This gorgeous little Christmas angel will add a heavenly touch to your festivities!

Method

Covering the Cakes

1. Stack all three cakes on top of each other, with the smallest at the top, and spread a little apricot glaze in between them to hold them together. Place the cakes off centre on the cake drum.

2. Working from top to bottom, cut away the cake using a sharp knife until you have achieved a cone shape.

3. Brush the cone with apricot glaze, cover with SK Marzipan and leave to dry for 24 hours.

Preparing the Halo

1. Cut a 24-gauge white floristry wire in half to create a piece approximately 15cm (6") long. Knead 10g ($^1/_3$oz) of White SFP then roll it into a thin sausage 12.5cm (5") long.

2. Dip the end of the wire into SK Edible Glue. Ease the end of the wire into the SFP and push it all the way through the length of the paste. Leave the ends of the wire showing.

3. Bring the two ends together and twist to secure them. Gradually work the SFP down the twisted wire so that it covers about 2.5cm (1"). Bend the circle of wire down by 90° and set aside to dry.

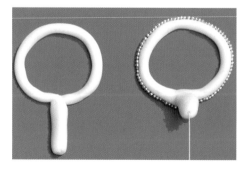

Body

1. Cover the cake with 400g (14oz) of white sugarpaste by wrapping the paste around the cone. Cut away the excess paste and smooth the join at the back with your fingertip.

2. Use the excess paste to cover the board around the angel. Crimp the paste all the way around the edge of the board using crimpers. Fix gold ribbon around the edge of the board using non-toxic stick glue, making sure the glue does not come into contact with the sugarpaste.

3. Reserve a tiny piece of white sugarpaste for the eyes and hair curl, then divide the remaining 100g ($3^1/_2$oz) of sugarpaste in half. Shape and mould two long triangles for the arms. Use a Dresden tool to mark creases in at the elbows. Fix the pointed end of the arms to the top of the cone and down the front of the gown.

4. Mark two panels down the front of the gown and the cuffs of the sleeves with the pointed end of a Dresden tool.

5. Make two hands from Flesh MMP.

Secure the hands in each sleeve with SK Edible Glue and then stick them together into a prayer position.

Collar

1. Roll out 20g ($^3/_4$oz) of White MMP and cut out two rings using a Garrett frill cutter. Cut through each one, keeping the paste in a circular shape.

2. Using the riveted end of the Dresden tool, frill along one edge of the paste. Bring the paste round to form a smaller circle, leaving a hole about 2.5cm (1") wide in the centre, and allow to overlap. Repeat with the second Garrett frill and place on top of the first. Dust the edges with SK Antique Gold Lustre Dust Colour.

3. Attach the finished collar to the top of the cake with SK Edible Glue. Adjust the ruffles as desired using the pointed end of the Dresden tool.

4. Push a dowelling rod through the cake from the centre hole of the angel's collar. Leave between 2.5cm and 5cm (1" and 2") protruding from the top to support the head.

Head

1. Brush the polystyrene ball with SK Edible Glue. Roll out 30g (1oz) of Flesh MMP and wrap this around the polystyrene ball, covering it completely. Carefully smooth the paste down to a point, then cut away the excess paste and smooth over the surface with the palms of your hands.

2. Position the covered ball over the dowelling rod and push down into the ruffled collar. You may need to smooth down areas of paste where pressure has been applied when putting the head into place.

3. For the mouth, use the wide end of a piping nozzle to indent a large smile on the angel's face.

4. Take a small amount of Flesh MMP for the nose, roll into a ball and stick in place with SK Edible Glue.

5. Roll two small balls of Flesh MMP for the ears, flatten slightly and gently push the smaller end of the ball tool into each one. Secure either side of the head with SK Edible Glue.

6. Colour a very small amount of the reserved white sugarpaste with SK Jet Black Paste Food Colour and make two small balls for eyes. Attach above the nose with SK Edible Glue.

Hair

1. Colour the tiny piece of white sugarpaste reserved earlier with SK Daffodil Paste Food Colour. Roll into a thin sausage and curl the end. Fix to the top of the head with SK Edible Glue.

2. Take the prepared halo and push into the back of the head until the wire has disappeared into the polystyrene.

Wings

1. Divide the remaining White MMP in half. Roll out the paste on a non-stick board and shape the wings, keeping the top curves thicker.

2. Using the larger end of the ball tool, make small, downward strokes from the thicker end to resemble feathers. Make them all the way to the base, letting the MMP take a natural shape.

3. Fix the wings to the back of the angel with SK Edible Glue, holding in place until they are secure.

4. Smooth down the join at the back so the wings look part of the gown.

To Finish

1. Gently dust down the front panels and sleeves of the gown with SK Antique Gold Lustre Dust using a small brush.

2. Brush a thin line of SK Edible Glue around the base of the angel. Carefully pick up the SK Mini Silver Balls with tweezers one-by-one and position on the line of glue.

3. Using the same method, add a line of silver balls around the front panels, sleeves, edges of each wing and the angel's halo.

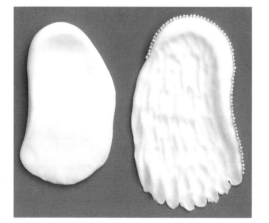

53

Carol Singers

Materials

15.5cm (6") round fruitcake

340g (12oz) SK Marzipan

500g (1lb 1oz) SK Royal Icing

SK Mexican Modelling Paste
(MMP): 180g (6oz) White

SK Paste Food Colour:
Poinsettia

SK Food Colour Pen:
Blackberry

SK Edible Glue

Raw spaghetti

Equipment

20.5cm (8") round cake drum

50cm (20") ribbon: white with
gold trim

Dresden tool (JC)

33-gauge floristry wires: white

Wire cutters

Method

Covering the Cake

Cover the cake with SK Marzipan and place centrally on the
drum. Leave to firm for 24 hours.

Choirboys

1. Whilst the marzipan on the cake is drying, model the
    choirboys for the cake top. Divide 90g (3oz) of White
    MMP into thirds and put two of the pieces to one side.

2. Working on the first choirboy, take off about a third of the
    paste for the head and hands and use the rest to roll a
    ball for the body. Elongate the ball, then round off the top
    and flatten the base.

3. Using the remaining piece of paste, roll two arms,
    elongate the top part
    and mark where the
    elbows will be using
    the pointed end of a
    Dresden tool. Fix the
    arms to the body
    with SK Edible Glue.

4. Roll a small round of
    paste for the collar
    and fix at the neck
    with SK Edible Glue.
    Insert a short length
    of raw spaghetti into
    the neck to support
    the head. Make the
    other two choirboys

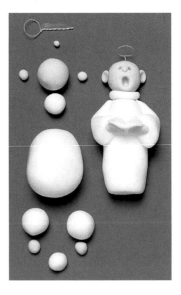

The beautiful sound of
choirboys singing carols fills
the air on a snowy evening,
creating the perfect atmosphere
for the seasonal festivities.

from the remaining 60g (2oz) of White MMP.

5. Colour the remaining MMP with a hint of SK Poinsettia Food Colour to make a pale pink shade. Divide the paste into three, one piece for each choirboy. Take off a pinch of paste for the ears, nose and hands and make the head from the remaining paste. Roll a ball for the head and push the paste over the spaghetti in the neck. Mark the eyes and mouth with a Dresden tool.

6. Roll tiny balls of paste for the ears and nose and secure in place with SK Edible Glue. Push the pointed end of the Dresden tool into the ears.

7. Make two hands and secure them into the ends of the sleeves. Overlap the hands to support the book.

8. Make a songbook for each of the choirboys by cutting out a rectangle of White MMP and indenting the spine down the centre with a knife. Carefully place the books in the hands of the choirboys and secure with SK Edible Glue.

9. To make the halos, cut a piece of 33-gauge floristry wire to approximately 7.5cm (3") long for each one. Wrap the wire around the top of the Dresden tool, then twist the ends together to form a loop. Bend the loop over then cut off the ends, leaving approximately 1.3cm (1/2") of twisted wire to push into the back of the head. As the wire has been inserted directly into the heads, ensure that the heads are removed completely before the cake is eaten.

Trees

Roll a cone of White MMP or sugarpaste and snip into the paste with fine scissors to form branches.

Snow

1. Mix up 500g (1lb 1oz) of SK Royal Icing. To give the icing a little more elasticity, 5ml (1 teaspoon) of glycerine per 500g pack can be added if required.

2. Using a palette knife, smooth the icing all over the cake and board. Beat the remaining icing to soft peak consistency and create peaks on the cake surface, leaving a flat area in the centre. Allow to dry.

To Finish

1. Position the choirboys and trees on top of the cake and secure in place using either SK Edible Glue or a little royal icing.

2. Draw details onto the choirboys and songbooks using an SK Blackberry Food Colour Pen.

3. Secure white ribbon around the edge of the board with a non-toxic glue stick.

56

Christmas Parcel

Materials

20.5cm (8") round fruitcake

500g (1lb 1oz) SK Marzipan

Sugarpaste: 150g (5oz) blue, 500g (1lb 1oz) cream

Small amount SK Royal Icing

SK Mexican Modelling Paste (MMP): 150g (5oz) Poppy

SK Sugar Florist Paste (SFP): 15g ($^1/_2$oz) Holly/Ivy, 10g ($^1/_3$oz) White

SK Paste Food Colour: Berberis

SK Dust Food Colours: Blackberry, Holly/Ivy

SK Food Colour Pen: Blackberry

SK Edible Glue

SK Confectioners' Glaze

Equipment

25.5cm (10") round cake drum

1m (40") blue ribbon

Large holly cutter (or template) (OP)

SK Great Impressions Medium Holly Veiner

Multi Ribbon Cutter (FMM)

Bone tool (PME)

Piping nozzle: no. 2

Piping bag

CelPad

Foam pieces

2cm ($^3/_4$") closed curved crimpers (PME)

Drinking straw

Greaseproof paper (optional)

Method
Covering the Cakes

1. Position the cake centrally on the cake drum. Glaze and marzipan the cake and set aside to dry.

2. Roll out the cream sugarpaste and cover the cake.

3. Using the back of a knife, indent approximately 2.5cm (1") down from the top of the cake to resemble a lid. To ensure the line is straight, you may wish to cut a strip of greaseproof paper to the height required and attach it around the cake whilst you work.

4. Roll out a long strip of blue sugarpaste and cover the

57

board around the cake. Trim to size, then crimp around the edge.

Label

1. Roll out 10g ($\frac{1}{3}$oz) of White SFP. Cut a label from the SFP and make a hole using the end of a drinking straw at the pointed end of the label.

2. Shape over a couple of foam pieces and leave to dry on a CelPad.

Ribbons

1. Roll out long lengths of Poppy MMP and cut long strips with the ribbon cutter. Use one large spacer and the straight edge wheels. Run the quilting wheel along both sides of the ribbon strip, to give the effect of stitching.

2. Attach two long lengths of ribbon to the parcel with SK Edible Glue, crossing them over at the centre and securing them down the sides. Cut away the base for a neat finish.

3. Cut the other ribbon lengths down to 7.5cm (3") pieces. Position a small piece of foam or rolled-up kitchen paper on the strip and using SK Edible Glue, stick the ends together over the foam to make a loop. Leave to dry. Make approximately twelve loops in the same way.

4. Fix the label to the top and side of the cake. Roll a long, thin sausage of White SFP, thread it through the label hole and attach to the ribbon in the centre of the cake with SK Edible Glue.

5. Write your chosen Christmas message onto the label using an SK Blackberry Food Colour Pen.

6. Brush some SK Edible Glue in the centre of the bow and position each loop in a circle, making sure four are at the top to cover the bases of the others.

To Finish

1. Add a hint of SK Berberis Paste Food Colour to a little SK Royal Icing to create a cream colour. Place a no. 2 piping nozzle in a piping bag and fill with icing. Pipe sets of three dots in a symmetrical pattern around the parcel.

2. For extra decoration, make two holly leaves from Holly/Ivy SFP, vein, dust and glaze. Add three berries made from Poppy MMP. Place the sprig on the board. (Detailed instructions for making holly can be seen on page 26.)

3. Attach blue ribbon around the edge of the cake drum with a non-toxic glue stick.

This parcel is a fairly quick
and easy cake to decorate
but once finished looks
good enough to open with
other Christmas presents!

Mini Gift Cakes

These miniature fruitcakes are ideal presents for someone special such as a grandparent and are great fun to make.

For each cake, glaze and marzipan a 10cm (4") round fruitcake (you will need approximately 150g/5oz of SK Marzipan). For the Christmas Pudding cake, you will need to trim around the base of the cake beforehand to create a more rounded shape. Place the cake onto a 15cm (6") round cake board, allow to dry overnight and then add the decoration of your choice following the instructions given.

Materials

Sugarpaste: 150g (5oz) blue

Small amount SK Royal Icing

SK Mexican Modelling Paste (MMP): 10g ($^1/_3$oz) Pale Mint, small amount Soft Apricot, small amount Sunshine, 50g (1$^3/_4$oz) White

SK Food Colour Pen: Blackberry

Equipment

Piping nozzle: no. 1

Piping bag

Snowman

Method

1. Cover the cake with blue sugarpaste and smooth the top and sides.

2. To make the tree, make a cone shape from the green sugarpaste and cut into the paste with fine scissors (as described in Snowboarding Snowmen, pages 10 to 13). Secure to the board with SK Edible Glue.

3. Make the snowman from White MMP (as described in Snowboarding Snowmen) and add a nose made from Soft Apricot MMP and a scarf made from Sunshine MMP. Secure the snowman to the board at the front of the cake.

4. Roll any left over blue sugarpaste into small balls and attach around the base of the cake using SK Edible Glue.

5. Pipe small dots on the cake to represent snow.

Christmas Pudding

Materials

Sugarpaste: 10g ($^1/_3$oz) chocolate, 50g (1$^3/_4$oz) cream, 100g (3$^1/_2$oz) white

SK Mexican Modelling Paste (MMP): 10g ($^1/_3$oz) Poppy

SK Sugar Florist Paste (SFP): 15g ($^1/_2$oz) Holly/Ivy

SK Paste Food Colour: Teddy Bear Brown

SK Edible Glue

SK Confectioners' Glaze

Equipment

Ball and bone tools (PME)

Method

1. Colour the white sugarpaste with SK Teddy Bear Brown Paste Food Colour. Roll out the paste into a long strip, long enough to go around the cake. Wrap the paste around the cake, making sure the sugarpaste is covering the cake at the bottom. Smooth the paste with your hands and join it together at the back. Cut away any excess paste at the top and bottom and smooth the surface again.

2. Make small indents randomly all over the cake with a ball and a bone tool.

3. Knead the chocolate sugarpaste until soft. Flatten several small balls of paste to represent currants and secure to the sides of the cake with SK Edible Glue.

4. Roll out the cream sugarpaste and gently pull out the edges with your fingers to make it look like it is running down the side of the pudding. Place over the top of the cake.

5. Complete the pudding by adding a sprig of holly (as described on page 26).

61

Christmas Parcel

Materials

Sugarpaste: 100g (3$^1/_2$oz) blue, 150g (5oz) pink

Small amount SK Royal Icing

SK Mexican Modelling Paste (MMP): 10g ($^1/_3$oz) Pale Mint, small amount Poppy, 10g ($^1/_3$oz) White

SK Food Colour Pen: Blackberry

SK Edible Glue

Equipment

Holly cutter (OP)

SK Great Impressions Medium Holly Veiner

Multi-ribbon cutter (FMM)

Piping nozzle: no. 1

Piping bag

Drinking straw

Method

1. Roll out the pink sugarpaste and cover the cake, smoothing down the top and the sides. Cut away any excess sugarpaste at the base.

2. Roll out the blue sugarpaste to form a long strip. Using the multi-ribbon cutter, place a spacer between the wavy edged wheels, cut two long strips measuring roughly 30.5cm (12"), two 7.5cm (3") strips and nine 5cm (2") strips.

3. Securing with SK Edible Glue, cross over the two longest lengths at the top and cut away neatly at the base. Cut an inverted 'V' into each of the 7.5cm (3") pieces, pinch the tops together and secure at the cross over.

62

4. Brush some SK Edible Glue on one end of each of the short pieces and join the ends together to make a loop. Secure the loops on top of the cake, making sure the centre is covered.

5. Roll out the White MMP and cut out a label shape. Use the end of a drinking straw to make a hole in the label. Roll out the remaining MMP to make the small loop of string and secure both the label and string into position on the cake.

6. Pipe small dots in groups of three around the sides of the cake using SK Royal Icing in a piping bag with a no. 1 nozzle.

7. Roll out the Pale Mint MMP and cut out three holly leaves. Vein in an SK Great Impressions Holly Veiner and secure into position at the front of the cake base with SK Edible Glue. Add some berries made from Poppy MMP.

8. Using an SK Blackberry Food Colour Pen, write your chosen festive message on the label.

Materials

200g (7oz) sugarpaste: white

Small amount SK Royal Icing

SK Mexican Modelling Paste (MMP): 10g (1/3oz) Pale Mint, small amount Poppy, 10g (1/3oz) Slate Grey, 10g (1/3oz) Soft Apricot

SK Paste Food Colour: Jet Black

SK Food Colour Pen: Blackberry

SK Edible Glue

Raw spaghetti

Equipment

SK Great Impressions Small Holly Veiner

Small holly cutter (OP)

Igloo and Penguin

Method

1. Cover the cake with 150g (5oz) of white sugarpaste and smooth down the top and the sides. Mark ice blocks all the way around the edge of the cake with the back of a knife.

2. Roll out 10g ($\frac{1}{3}$oz) of white sugarpaste to a rectangle 2.5cm x 7.5cm (1" x 3") and again mark ice blocks over the top. Bend into an arch and secure to the front of the cake.

3. Spread some SK Royal Icing on the board around the base of the cake and in the doorway of the igloo. Roll small balls of white sugarpaste and push them into the royal icing.

4. Make small holly leaves and berries from Pale Mint and the Poppy MMP using the same method as in the Christmas Parcel. Secure to the igloo with SK Edible Glue.

5. To make the penguin, divide the Soft Apricot MMP into three. Roll out two pieces for the feet, flatten and make three indentations for toes on each.

6. Make a pear shape from about 10g ($\frac{1}{3}$oz) of white sugarpaste for the body. Secure on top of the feet with SK Edible Glue.

7. Add some SK Jet Black Paste Food Colour to the Slate Grey MMP to make black. Roll out the paste and cut a kite shape. Pull the top corner over the penguin's head, secure with SK Edible Glue and position the wings.

8. Make a beak from the last piece of Soft Apricot MMP. Shape it into a triangle, secure in place with SK Edible Glue and mark two nostrils with the end of a raw spaghetti stick.

9. Mark on the eyes with an SK Blackberry Food Colour Pen and position the penguin on the cake board beside the igloo.